Ten Laws of Great Decision-Making

Beating the odds in Business

Oliver Surdival

Published on Kindle Direct Publishing

Publication Date: January 2020

Author photograph by Martin Kuzmicz

Sold by: Amazon

ISBN- 9781673597448

For Lorraine, Arron, Shannon and Dylan

"It does not take much strength to do things, but it requires great strength to decide on what to do."

– Elbert Hubbard

Thank you

To my family, for enduring and supporting me over the last several months of hearing about "Great-Decision making…"

To Victor del Rosal, colleague and friend, for your support and thorough review, I love you man.

To Michael Callaghan, mentor, advisor and friend who has been on this journey with me from the start, sincere thanks.

To Siofra McDonagh, colleague and friend, for your support and thorough review, thank you.

About the Author

Oliver Surdival

Oliver Surdival is a technologist, entrepreneur and investor with over two decades of experience leading teams in successful businesses. Oliver sits on various boards, advising and helping companies to achieve their profitability and growth ambitions by enabling the board, management and leadership team to make great decisions consistently.

Oliver started his first technology company developing software back in 2005, which was acquired five years later. He soon founded his second start-up tech company in 2010, which was acquired in 2018.

Oliver lives in the west of Ireland and is married with three beautiful children. He is passionate about creating jobs and opportunities for the people in the west of Ireland and has invested in many start-ups, giving his time for free to help and advise businesses in the west to expand.

Content

Foreword

Oliver Surdival represents the rare breed of senior business leaders and entrepreneurs who can build, scale and sell their business in the midst of a global recession while living and working in the West of Ireland. This book is essential reading for anyone who wishes to understand the underlying laws of great decision-making and how great decision-making can catapult your business or career.

However, this is not only a book for entrepreneurs, but it is also a must-read for business leaders, managers and decision-makers in Europe and the Americas, especially for those who wish to build and scale a successful business with high-performance teams.

In a highly accessible manner, Oliver has managed to define and break down the key laws of great decision-making that has helped him throughout his career. Oliver gives a highly compelling account of what it takes to make great decisions as an entrepreneur, manager or senior business leader to grow your business.

I hope, dear reader, that you find the laws as enjoyable and useful as I did. It is an enlightening journey of innovation with highly valuable lessons learned for decision-makers in to-days world.

Victor del Rosal

Founder of Emtechub, emerging technology education startup,
Author of Disruption: Emerging Technologies & the Future of Work

Introduction

At around 2:30 pm on November first, 2018, on a sunny afternoon in the West of Ireland, I signed the dotted line and just like that, it became official—I had sold my technology service business, bringing to a close my 7-year journey and giving way to a new and exciting chapter in my life.

Throughout my journey of building successful businesses over many years, I have given much thought as to why some businesses in the same industry succeed while others fail, given that they have the same access to markets, finance and talent. The only logical conclusion is in the decisions those businesses made. I began to develop laws and frameworks to act as my north star to guide me in making great decisions and improve the chances of success.

What you will read in this book extracts is not only my decision-making experience and the laws of great decision-making in the business world but the experience of numerous other entrepreneurs and senior business leaders from diverse industries globally. It is a research-based approach that identifies and distils *what works* in great decision-making.

In each chapter, I discuss how I applied each of the *ten Laws of Great Decision-Making* to build, grow and ultimately sell my tech company in Ireland, while managing to survive various challenges, including the financial crisis.

Whether you intend to build a lifestyle business or scale your business to sell it, the underlying assumption is that you build a business that is attractive to your key stakeholders, including investors. I share a decision-making approach that you can adapt to suit your own pursuits.

I sincerely hope that after reading, reflecting and applying the *Ten Laws of Great Decision-Making* you will find yourself in a much better position to make great decisions and that you will apply some of these ideas to build, scale and—if you choose to—sell your company. I wish you every success as you carve your path to great decision-making.

Oliver Surdival
January 2020

- CHAPTER 1 -

Know your reason to fly
Understand your motivations

*"It is not enough to be industrious; so are the
ants. What are you industrious about?"*
–Henry David Thoreau

In 1898 Samuel Pierpont Langley was given 50 thousand dollars by the US War Department to build a flying machine. He was a highly respected and award-winning scientist who became the third secretary of the Smithsonian Institute. "Langley was obsessed with his place in science history," reports Liane Hansen for National Public Radio. Langley had already built an impressive career as an astronomer, but he also wanted to "make a discovery on a par with Alexander Graham Bell and Thomas Edison".

After years of work, in 1903, Langley was finally ready to test his flying machine. For the highly anticipated day, October 7 of that year, reporters swarmed the top of a houseboat on the Potomac River, and when Langley launched his aerodrome... it crashed straight into the river.

A second attempt two months later, on December 8, 1903, the trial also failed when Langley's model shooting straight up, then plummeting back into the water.

The Wright Brothers

Not far from there, two unknown brothers were conducting their own attempts at a flying machine, partly inspired in Langley's work and funded with the proceeds of their bicycle shop. On December 17, 1903, just nine days after Langley's second failed attempt, and the Wright brothers successfully performed the first controlled manned flight in history.

To Langley's lament and despite his excellent reputation and his resources, he was unable to finish first in the race to build a flying machine.

Langley's reason to fly

While it can be argued that several factors connected to patenting and funding came into play in the Langley-Wright rivalry, there are several legitimate questions that could be asked:

Could Langley have used his contacts to advance the industry *after* his failed attempts? Could he have come up with new patents of his own? Based on his connections and resources, could he have established partnerships to improve his design work? Should Langley have continued despite the setbacks? Had Langley finished first, would he have continued engagement with the budding flight industry? And perhaps most importantly, why didn't Langley think it was worthwhile to continue working on his flying machine despite the setbacks? Could he have successfully fought the Wright brothers to keep the patent in his name?

Based on historical records, one can assume that Langley's primary motivation had to do with his reputation and standing in the scientific community and perhaps with the possibility of becoming a significant government contractor. These are legitimate aspirations, but as we will review, they can get in the way of actually solving challenges. It seems he was more obsessed with how others would regard him than on building a machine that could fly. Based on his actions before and after December 1903 we may conclude that he cared more about finishing first in the race to perform the world's first manned flight as opposed to building or perfecting a machine that could work thereafter.

In a twist of historical fate, after Langley's death in 1906, it turned out that his aerodrome was indeed capable of making short manned flights over a lake—after modifications were made. To this day Langley holds an esteemed place in history—the Langley Air Force Base and the USS Langley among many other buildings and ships were named after him.

The first law of great decision-making is to understand your motivations and reasons for making decisions in the first place. It points towards open self-examination to help you understand and achieve your goals.

LAW #1:

KNOW YOUR DRIVE FOR DECISION-MAKING

Why Law #1?

The entrepreneur or senior business leader who understands their drivers to make great decisions will not only have the *motivation* but a powerful *why* underpinning ability to guide their decision choices.

This sense of purpose will help decision-makers endure and seek out the best solutions when the going gets tough. Decision-makers who know *why* exactly they are doing things will have a compass to guide their decision-making process.

My reasons to fly

At the start of my journey, which had many ups and downs; I had a burning ambition to build something special and grow a successful business. At my core, I had a calling, a sense of purpose to create job opportunities for the people in the west of Ireland. This is my fundamental reason to fly which affects many of my investment decisions and businesses that I devote my personal time too.

Before CloudStrong, I ran a small software development company, designing and building software applications with a remote team. It was an extremely happy and exciting period of my life as an entrepreneur.

Back in 2010, I first heard the word cloud as a platform to deliver IT infrastructure and services which piqued my interest considerably; all the signs indicating it would become the Next Big Thing. I immediately started to investigate the cloud opportunity to see if there was a market trend I could take advantage of. Having a background in IT and software development, I was quite comfortable to invest in a startup business that would focus on delivering cloud solutions. Just before I set up my cloud business, I got a lucky break when an existing client asked if we did cloud to which I quickly replied: "Of course, what are you looking for?" My seminal client needed email and a web-based collaborative platform, which we delivered. That was in 2011, I sold my software development business to fund my new startup, and that's how CloudStrong got started.

Decision-makers face challenges all the time

The message for me is that, in your professional life, if you want to be an effective decision-maker, you must first recognise and accept that you are in that position to make decisions. You will be faced with challenges that may be relatively simple to solve, while others can and will become more complex issues. But the one thing you cannot do is anticipate and expect smooth sailing. You must accept the fact that your life as a decision-maker will be full of all sorts of challenges. That, in essence, is your reason for being a decision-maker—to solve those challenges. But all of this does come at a price. Business problems may and will stress you and may keep you up at night, and this is especially the case if you are not expecting them. The life of the decision-maker does come at a price, and this must be accounted for *before* you start.

Lifestyle or exit strategy

Another aspect of decision-making in business, especially in the context of startups, has to do with understanding your overall game plan, knowing what your business pursuit actually is: are you aiming to develop a lifestyle business, organically building a practice as a specialist, or are you looking to launch and sell (exit) your business?

There is no right or wrong answer to the above, but the ramifications of these strategies will impact your decision-making criteria. One path may allow you to live and work on your own terms requiring, for example, no outside investment, while the other may imply working with several stakeholders throughout the process, as well as requiring external investment and shared decision-making. The different scenarios may or may not suit your aspirations.

When I look back at the decisions, I have made with previous businesses; it is clear that I could have opted for a lifestyle business concentrating all of the decision-making around me. However, I decided to create instead, *systems* that would help us scale and serve more customers. We kept focusing on building systems to deliver significant value and ultimately returns for investors. A lifestyle business, on the other hand, is typically harder to invest in because the principal asset is a person—the business only makes money if the owner/founder is actively engaged in it. Again, there is no right or wrong answer as to what approach is best for you. It depends on what works for your particular set of circumstances as each path carries its own complexities. However, the decision must be made sooner rather than later.

Your own reasons

While no one is guaranteed success in a business endeavour, in my experience the one thing that business decision-makers are guaranteed to face are *challenges*, lots of challenges and decisions to make, regularly. These challenge you, the decision-maker, with a varying degree of complexity, uncertainty and importance. In light of this, it is essential to understand what it is you are ultimately trying to achieve. Law #1 asks you to consider "your purpose for decision-making".

How you respond to Law #1 will likely determine if you will stick to a particular business idea or if you will move on looking for alternative paths. Your purpose will determine the value of the outcomes along the way, and in light of this, you will know what is and isn't essential.

Knowing your purpose and reasons is not an absolute judgment concerning what is good or bad for anyone in your situation, but a relative one, that pertains to you. The point is that it will be helpful to be clear on what your ultimate goal is, to remind you and carry you through the ups and downs of decision-making.

The power of purpose

The Oxford dictionary defines purpose as "the reason for which something is done or created or for which something exists."

According to researchers Patrick E. McKnight and Todd B. Kashdan in "Purpose in Life as a System that Creates and Sustains Health and Well-Being: An Integrative, Testable Theory", purpose is a cognitive process that defines life goals and provides personal meaning. They posit that devoting effort and making progress toward life goals provides a significant, renewable source of engagement and meaning. Purpose, they postulate, offers a testable, causal system that synthesizes outcomes including life expectancy, satisfaction, and mental and physical health.

What is relevant for a decision-maker is that "such outcomes may be explained best by considering the motivation of the individual—a motivation that comes from having a purpose". In contrast, a decision-maker *without* a purpose may not have the same level of energy to carry out his or her work, or to see it through to the end, which is useful in explaining the differences between Samuel Pierpont Langley and the Wright Brothers.

Knowing your reasons to fly *before* you embark on a journey can be a source of sustained energy to propel flight, especially in turbulent times.

- CHAPTER 2 -

Mark the spot

Define X before you solve for it

"Judge a man by his questions rather than by his answers." —Voltaire.

The *SS Central America*, also known as the Ship of Gold, was an 85-metre sidewheel steamer that operated between Central America and the eastern coast of the United States during the 1850s. On September 3, 1857, close to six hundred passengers and crew sailed from Colón, Panamá for New York loaded with over 9 tons of gold. On September 9, the ship encountered a Category 2 hurricane off the coast of the Carolinas. Within three days, in what turned out to be one of the worst disasters of its era, the *SS Central America* would lie at the bottom of the sea with 423 souls lost—fortunately, hundreds were rescued. But the ship also took down with it gold worth a modern-day equivalent of $292 million, causing shockwaves in the financial system and contributing to the Panic of 1857.

The precise spot where the ship sank—and where the gold was to be found—remained a mystery for over *one hundred and thirty years*. It became an obsession for generations of treasure hunters challenged with knowing where exactly to look.

To find the treasure first know where to look

In 1985 a multi-disciplinary team called the Columbus America Discovery Group set out to locate the shipwreck and recover the gold.

At its disposal were the latest technologies including sonar, robotics, fibre optics, high-resolution scanning and unmanned submersibles. Despite these advanced technologies, the first step in finding the treasure consisted of a *theory,* a rather novel approach to shipwreck searching.

High-level mapping: Bayesian search theory

According to Bayesian search theory, the procedure for locating shipwrecks starts with the formulation of as many reasonable hypotheses as possible regarding the fate of the object. For each hypothesis, a probability cloud for the location of the object is generated. This leads to a function giving the chances of actually finding an object in location X. For objects underwater, this also depends on water depth—the shallower the water, the higher the chances of finding the shipwreck; conversely the probability of success decreases in deeper water.

The next step consists of combining the above information to render an overall probability density map, resulting in the probability of finding the shipwreck by looking in location X, for all possible locations. This can be visualized as a *contour map of probability*. With it, the team would start the search in the areas of highest probability.

Based on research papers from the 1857 disaster, this approach was followed by the Columbus-America Discovery Group, covering an area of over 3,600 square kilometres. And in 1988 the team found success—they were finally able to pinpoint the location of the *SS Central America* to a spot 257 kilometres off Charleston, South Carolina and successfully recovered an estimated $100 to $150 million in gold.

To find the business opportunity first know where to look

As a business decision-maker, you know there is a business opportunity somewhere in front of you, and while it is tempting to think it could be within reach, the real trick is knowing where exactly to look. To unlock the treasure, one of the keys is understanding the precise nature of the business challenge you are addressing so that you can focus your resources on solving it. Hence, to find the treasure, it is central to first pinpoint its precise location, that is, to clearly define it.

LAW #2:

CLEARLY DEFINE THE CHALLENGE YOU ARE TRYING TO SOLVE

Why Law #2?

A business challenge that is not well defined is an issue or problem that is understood by no one, or even worse, interpreted in conflicting ways.

Once all the relevant stakeholders agree on what exactly it is that you are tackling you can start to devise the solutions that are relevant to the particular challenge in question.

Likewise, a challenge that is broadly defined tends to waste implementation resources.

Hence, your decision-making ability will be more effective if you clearly frame and define the challenge in a clear, concise manner.

Find your X

One of the most useful pieces of advice for founders and senior business leaders could be distilled as: *know thy customer* and *define the nature of the challenge your customer is facing*.

In my case, from the start, we aimed to understand our customers' pain points. Once we were able to understand our customers' needs, we were in a much better position to design solutions and services that tackled those challenges. Once we were clear on the definition of the specific challenges faced by our customers, we were able to start building solutions and services that they wanted to buy.

Study the challenge first

The lesson for me was to identify the specific challenges faced by my prospective clients before trying to sell them a service. Despite our strengths in cloud computing, we did not have a business until we recognised how we could specifically add value. The business *opportunity* started for us once it was clear that our customers faced *challenges* and that we were in a position to help.

One of the easy mistakes to make as an entrepreneur is to put more emphasis on your own services while overlooking customers' actual needs. In other words, your strengths can become a distraction if they are not correctly aimed at addressing customer pain points, regardless of how cutting-edge your technology is. While this may sound counter-intuitive, I learned that you only have a business if you can solve a challenge for a customer. Once you have clearly defined the customer's challenge and *everyone agrees on the nature of the challenge*—that is, you have clearly defined what X is and where it is— you will be in a position to make great decisions and propel your business forward.

Seek constructive feedback

If you've already built a working prototype, seek as much feedback as possible, especially regarding negative customer experience. It is only human to seek approval and to feel good by knowing how well you are doing, but the moment of truth happens when you actively look for things that *don't* work.

When a customer is compelled to leave a negative review, it might be too late; they might be on the way out the door. So, don't ignore negative reviews, but even better, be proactive in seeking real, honest feedback as early and as often as possible. And always be open for sceptical users who may question your intentions or may disagree or not like you altogether. That is fine. You may learn something from these users and know that it is OK to disagree.

Proactively seeking negative feedback is another way of finding that high priority X—this search approach could lead you to the discovery of opportunities which you had never envisioned and which could yield high returns if addressed correctly.

Get out of the building but don't prototype yet

Don't expect to find your X sitting behind your computer all the time, it is vital to get out of the building and talk to your current and potential customers. Otherwise, someone else might do it while you are busy solving for a problem which may be irrelevant or a non-issue to your user base. Ask people what might work best for them and understand their real-world scenarios.

You should not prototype first and ask questions later—build your prototype around the feedback you receive, then prototype. Tweaks can be made or the whole idea re-designed at a relatively low cost and risk, but it should all start centred on real conversations with your customers.

If you are stuck for ideas on where to look, be alert to challenges that annoy your current or prospective clients. Ask them what it is they hate in their particular domain or industry.

Don't narrow down the possibilities

When identifying opportunity be careful not to let others inadequately frame your thoughts and narrow the options. This typically happens when people ask you to decide in binary terms (yes or no, black or white, up or down?) or when certain assumptions are introduced but not called out. It is essential to clarify the assumptions so that you are not needlessly narrowing down your options or choosing from an artificially limited range of options. Be ready to spot these reduced frames of thought that restrict your decision-making ability.

In data we trust

To know where X is, study the challenge, see how people are coping, what solutions they are currently using. Do as much homework as you can to really place yourself in the user's shoes. Understand the pain points and *feel* the pain. The better you can do this; the more efficient your solution will be.

While a refined intuition is essential for a seasoned manager, decision-making has to be informed by data. It is not enough to make decisions that "feel right", decision-making must be backed by data with a mix of primary and secondary research, that is, user insights and published research, if applicable. As a rule of thumb, I would say that proximity to your refined customer segment and users is the best source of validation.

Find X first before you solve for it

In summary, before you set out to make decisions, conduct thorough research until you are satisfied that you know who your customer is and the nature of the issue they are facing.

As a founder or senior business leader, it is very tempting to solve the problem even before you have heard all the facts. It is imperative to survey the landscape and get a detailed map before you attempt to go for the treasure.

Otherwise, you may solve the wrong issues: you may waste resources addressing the issues that are not urgent or that will yield lower returns. This is because the problem is incorrectly defined. Great decision-making is about solving challenges, but more importantly, it's about solving the right ones first.

And when you do this, it is hard not to get excited about the whole process, once you realise that you are building something that matters.

CHAPTER 3

Don't sell refrigerators

Identify the true value of what you sell

"Try not to become a man of success. Rather become a man of value."—Albert Einstein

On February 10, 1806, an American entrepreneur by the name of Frederic Tudor sent off a ship bound for the Caribbean island of Martinique from Boston harbour, loaded with 80 tons of a unique kind of cargo. Tudor attempted something unprecedented—sell ice to the islanders. Despite concerns that the ice would melt on its way, it arrived in Martinique in perfect condition. But Tudor had a more pressing problem—no one would buy it. Even with his best marketing attempts, the oppressive Caribbean heat was not enough reason to persuade users to buy ice.

Despite the setback, this brave endeavour marked the start of the natural ice trade, a 19th-century and early-20th-century industry, which centred on the east coast of the United States and Norway. It involved the large-scale harvesting, transportation and sale of ice that came from nature. Over time the consumption of ice became a household practice, and Tudor would play a big role in it in the coming three decades; he went on to ship about 12 thousand tons of ice around the world (including Martinique), earning the title of *Ice King*.

Ice, Inc.

The ice trade involved cutting vast chunks of ice from frozen lakes and streams and transporting them down rivers. This led to the construction of substantial wooden storage houses along rivers, with capacities of 5 to 80 thousand tons of ice as well as thick insulation to keep them cool during the summer.

Logistically speaking, man-power evolved to mule and horse-power and then to steam-powered conveyors and elevators, along with increasingly sophisticated slanted tracks to swiftly move blocks of ice in and out of storage houses.

The product would be transported by ship, barge or railroad to its final destination around the world. Networks of ice wagons were typically used to distribute the ice to domestic and commercial customers. In parts of the US, it was up to the *iceman* to deliver it just like any other delivery (milk, post, newspaper, etc.)

The ice trade became a large-scale, multi-million dollar operation spanning the production, shipping and retail of ice for use in industrial, household and other commercial applications. By 1847, over 50 thousand tons of natural ice travelled by ship or train to twenty-eight cities across the United States.

By this stage, it was clear that consumers had placed a high value on a clear identifiable benefit: being able to keep their food and drink cold.

Ice 2.0: ice factories

By the mid-1850s a series of patents led to commercial refrigeration, paving the way for the mass production of ice, labelled *artificial* ice to distinguish it from ice that occurred naturally.

Homes were fitted with *iceboxes*, a household appliance developed in 1861, and ice blocks would be slipped into them. By 1868, the world's first commercial ice plant opened and by the 1910s people had discovered the numerous uses for manufactured ice and plants opened all over the US. At this stage, ice had become a commodity.

Despite the evolving technology, for consumers, the fundamental benefit remained constant: being able to keep their food and drink cold.

Ice 3.0: the personal ice maker

In 1916 the Kelvinator became one of the first refrigerators for home and domestic to be introduced in the US. By 1925 it gave users the first self-contained refrigeration unit with the cooling system, compressor and condenser in one cabinet. More importantly, it marked a key point in the evolution of the ice trade that brought ice-making into homes. What began with the painstaking production of natural ice and continued with the manufacturing of artificial ice in factories, culminated with the production of ice *at home*.

With this third generation of the ice trade, the complex logistics of producing ice, including the delivery by an icemen was made redundant—now families could make their own ice. But the fundamental benefit remained the same: the ability to keep food and drink cold.

Moreover, the movers and shakers of each ice trade generation tended to conduct business as usual as opposed to openly embracing the transition to the next generation. This was arguable because they had already invested considerable resources—they had their own way of doing things—making it difficult to divest and move on to the next generation. But more importantly, perhaps it was the inertia of the *status quo* that prevented them from seeing what customers really wanted.

The how or the what?

From the point of view of the consumer you are not in the business of cutting and transporting ice from lakes, making ice in factories or even making household refrigerators, you are in the business of *chilling* their food and drink. At the end of the day, your customer doesn't care *how* you do things as long as you do them in a way that suits their needs.

In retrospect, one can logically connect these dots across ice generations and easily separate the product from the mode of production, that is, distinguish the *what* from the *how*. But it is not as easy if you are *in* it.

The brief history of the ice trade reminds us that as a decision-maker, you're not in the business of selling things but instead of delivering benefits. If there's a better way to provide such value, your customers will sooner or later embrace it, so you might as well embrace it now.

However, for the players, it may not be as simple. Decision-makers each had their own way of making ice, and it probably became not only their business but a way of life. It was arguably challenging to profitably transition from one generation to the next. Your professional identity would be closely tied to *how* you did things.

But as we will explore, problems in decision-making arise when the *how* is prioritised over the *what*, when the decision-maker loses sight of the *value* to be added.

LAW #3:

FOCUS ON ADDING VALUE AND SOLVING THE RIGHT CHALLENGE

Why Law #3?

Decision-making ultimately concerns itself with the achievement of goals and the value-added to the customer, which justifies being in business.

It cares about the *what*—the actual benefits that stakeholders receive—as opposed to *how* these are delivered, assuming that the delivery model makes business sense.

If the customer perceives that the business does not deliver enough value over alternatives, that business offerings will tend to be replaced.

The decision-maker ought to separate the means of creating value from the actual value delivered to the customer. This implies letting go of inefficient ways of doing things, so that customer's value is maximised.

The peril of falling in love with *your solution*

While the ice trade evolved over a hundred years spanning three distinctive tech generations, today these shifts may happen in less than 12 months. One of the difficulties in decision-making comes from clinging on to a particular technology or way of doing business while losing sight of the customer. It's very easy to fall in love with the technology or idea you're pitching to the point that you forget that it's all about solving challenges.

At the end of the day, customers really don't care about your solution; they care about their problems. The emphasis must be placed on listening to their needs as the central piece of the equation.

Don't build a solution looking for a problem

What happens if you build the solution first and then look for customer pain points? John Delano, co-founder and CEO of Saltbox, warns to "always focus on solving a real business challenge... Avoid getting caught up in designing a cool app that needs to find a challenge," he says.

Perhaps the hardest challenge may not be technical but to really understand the evolving needs of the customer. For us, it is clear that we must continually talk to our customers, whether it's on the road or on the phone. The decision-maker ought to speak to key stakeholders to genuinely understand the challenges faced. This puts you in a much better position to come up with solutions appropriate to the stated needs.

Add value with the customer in mind

To truly add value first, you need to cater to the actual needs and problems of your customers. This is the desirability criteria. If you don't, you are wasting your time building a product nobody wants.

The second criterion is technical feasibility: are you able to build and deliver your solution? This is where you need to be careful to fulfil your promises or don't promise something you cannot deliver.

Finally, for financial viability, you must ensure that your cost structure is low enough to allow for healthy margins after all costs have been considered.

Paying customers will stick with you as long as you add value to them. Focus on what *they* have to say to you. However, often times this implies consciously excluding certain segments. It is too easy to get distracted, chasing new opportunities without really focusing on your most promising niche.

Validate your prototype

Validation is not testing code or asking your co-founder if you think your solution is the right one. Validating an idea is getting your *early adopters* or critical stakeholders to try out your solution. They must agree to be completely honest with their feedback so that you can learn from their own experience.

While a refined intuition is essential for a seasoned manager, decision-making has to be informed by data. It is not enough to make decisions that "feel right", the decision-maker must be able to back data with a mix of primary and secondary research, that is, user insights and published research, if applicable.

By definition, early adopters are not concerned if the earliest version of your solution does not have all the bells and whistles you could hope for. In fact, you should be able to deliver a clean but simple version in the understanding that more robust features will be available further down the line. What matters is that you are providing a solution that hits the spot; you are indeed solving for X.

Not in the business of selling *things*

We keep reminding ourselves that we are not in the cloud business, but that we offer services to help our customers get their own work done. Rather than focusing on our technology, we understand we are in the business of making their work experience easier. We are not in the business of selling products or services; we are here to add value.

We are not overly concerned about *selling* in the traditional sense, but rather in building the product and *sharing* our solution to the right users. The shift here is to genuinely attempt to solve our users' particular needs.

When you empathise and feel their pain, it is easier to direct your energies to build and deploy solutions that quench that pain. Then it becomes unacceptable not to share the solution that you created with a growing customer base. If you follow this logic, you are *not selling*; you are helping, you are adding value by sharing a solution.

Early adopters are evangelists

One of the upsides of making this whole approach the right way is that you are genuinely passionate about adding value to your users; they will become natural evangelists for your company. Over the years, word of mouth advertising has been vital for us. The close relationships we have built with our customers over the years have fortunately paid off in unsolicited referrals. By focusing on adding value, we have progressively earned trust in opening doors with new customers.

Bridging tech generations

In our case, from a service delivery perspective, it turned out that it was relatively quick and easy to deploy cloud services since the hardware and software could be supported and managed by our cloud vendor. The back-end cost structure was efficient, in terms of price and speed of delivery which included tech support. In the first few months, I validated that there was a solid need in the market and that our solution was both feasible and viable. I now had the beginning of a profitable business model; all I needed was to add services and customers.

With that said over time, the underlying technologies powering our business have kept changing, and we have continuously adapted to sustain or increase our value offering. We remind ourselves that our users don't care how things get done in the backend; they care about the value that gets delivered at the right price.

At the end of the day, the decision-maker will stay relevant in proportion to the value-added to their customers, regardless of the particular technology used.

- CHAPTER 4 -

Build like a weaver bird

Limit your risks building iteratively

"Follow your passion, assuming it involves building products that solve real problems." — Ram Singh, Gazeable.

Weaver birds have a fascinating ability to build nests; they can be spotted carrying long blades of grass to their chosen destination and then artistically weaving them together while these are still fresh. As time passes, the sun dries the green grass, and the nest hardens. The way they build is remarkable for such a tiny creature, weighing in at around 25 to 50 grams (a golf ball weighs 46 grams) and measuring between 14 to 20 centimetres, weaver birds demonstrate their skill as true artisans of nature; some are able to weave a nest in less than a day.

Once a nest is completed it is quality-inspected typically by the female to see if it is accepted as the future home for the little chicks. If it passes the test, it becomes a brood nest, but if it doesn't the nest must be destroyed, and the process started over again. Nest building is a crucial skill for weaver birds as they must offer protection from predators, including snakes. Weaver birds must learn to create a nest, so they are often seen practising.

Furthermore, there is a particular type of weaver bird endemic to South Africa, Namibia, and Botswana called the *social* weaver bird. It is especially noteworthy because it is one of the few birds that build extensive compounds.

Just like for any other weaver bird, each nest is built and quality-inspected, with the peculiarity that nests are clustered resulting in magnificent compounds. Some sociable weaver nests weigh several *tons* and can get so heavy that they knock down the tree they are perched on. The largest sociable weaver nests are over 6 metres wide and about 3 metres tall. These compounds can consist of around 100 nesting chambers providing a home for up to 400 birds, and they are built to last— some nests have been habited by generations of sociable weaver for over 100 years. These are indeed the largest tree nests in the world and perhaps the most remarkable structures built by any bird. A weaver bird—especially a social weaver bird—may look like an ordinary little songbird, but it is, in fact, a surprisingly skilled builder.

The importance of starting small

The weaver bird's example provides a clue for decision-makers. While there is constant pressure in the business world to make great decisions that translate into sustained and growing profit, weaver birds remind decision-makers of the importance of starting small, ensuring that the first prototype you build or idea you put forward meets the quality requirements of your stakeholders.

A single project or prototype that meets your customer's expectations can be (and typically is) the start of any business. While it's great to have a vision and to think big, the focus must be on getting it right *for the first time*. That's how I have conducted my business over the years—starting small, then building successively.

LAW #4:

LIMIT THE RISK OF YOUR DECISIONS

Why Law #4?

To determine if a decision (idea, project, product, service) will add value to stakeholders, before rolling out at a large scale, the decision must be tested as a smaller experiment.

This approach will considerably mitigate the risks associated with decision-making.

Furthermore, the test will help the decision-maker learn and perfect the product or service, crucially, including feedback from key stakeholders.

Addressing your stakeholders' needs

Since great decision-making involves managing your opportunity costs and taking risks, it is a wise idea to limit your potential losses while learning the most from your business experiment. Whether you are running the show as your own boss or working with other senior leaders, great decision-makers use resources wisely to maximise return on investment, typically with a long-term view.

"Don't spend a dime until you have a prototype that you take to a potential customer who states he would either buy or subscribe to a monthly charge to use it. Now get it out and begin collecting data that can help you adjust," agrees David Jennings, eVenues founder and CEO.

Stay focused and *exclude* customers

What we did in our early days was to stay focused on no more than one or two customer segments at a time, adding value once we had gathered enough feedback. We then built solutions that were specifically relevant to those users. For us, it was often tempting to go chasing new segments. This would have become a distraction from core segments that were starting to work well for us.

The tricky part here is knowing when and how to exclude large segments of potential customers who do not have an urgent need for your solution. In other words, you must decide to say *no* to those customers for whom you are not ready for just yet. This is usually easier said than done; the temptation is to serve everyone. What this means in practice is that you should work with the customers that almost desperately need your solution. It's a win-win scenario when you find a customer who has the highest level of urgency.

The point is that staying focused helps you build your capabilities, and progressively roll out new features. As you keep improving your offering, you come to a point where you can increasingly automate processes, and that frees you up to go looking for new profitable niches—not unlike the social weaver bird, building the compound, one chamber at a time.

The 20,000 user problem

Beware of being sidetracked by secondary issues which get in the way of actually making a decision or addressing the primary concern. If you identified the most critical challenges to solve, prioritise these before moving on. Focus on the task at hand and don't give in to solving problems that do not need to be solved at that particular stage.

I remember a time sitting down with my senior management team, discussing how we would bring a particular solution to market that would generate significant revenue for the business. The discussions were going well, and the team had excellent ideas until someone asked how we would be able to offer technical support once we achieved our target of 20,000 users. At that moment, we should have noticed the key operative word: *once*, but we didn't. The team attention and focused switched from imminent rollout to solving a problem we did not have and did not need to answer at that time. We agreed to meet in one week to give people time to reflect on the issue. I was very frustrated that we could not make progress on the rollout of the new service and I started to analyse what had happened. At the next meeting, there was a great and engaging discussion on how we could solve the problem to support 20,000 plus users. And then I asked the question: *how long would it actually take the business to acquire 20,000 users?* The answer was 12 months after launch. I then asked the team, where should our focus be, on the role out of the services or solving a challenge we might have in 12 months if we reached our goal. My team saw that we got distracted and the discussion at that moment ended, and we came back to discussing operations for service deployment, but not after having exhausted ourselves with an irrelevant debate. We had mistakenly focused on solving a problem we did not have, instead of aiming to solve the task at hand. We would address the 20,000 user support challenge when the time came.

To make great decisions or solve a problem, it is important to address the correct problem. Be aware of people framing your thought process as it is an easy trap to fall into. It can happen very easily and can catch out even the most experienced decision-makers.

Broad or niche?

You may also wonder if you should research a broad range of customer segments or if you should pick a specific one to narrow down your focus.

What we discovered is that while you may start with a broad scope in mind, the chances of success increase if you concentrate on a narrower segment and type of challenge. That is, you should look broadly for opportunities, but once you are confident that you have found a promising niche, you should focus on it.

Later, in the design stage, you may be again tempted to design for "everyone", to keep your options open. However, the issue with this approach is that your offerings may turn out to be bland, generic and ultimately unappealing to most of the users, that is, you design for *everyone* but for *no one* at the same time.

"Niche out your product... the more you try to do early on, the harder it will be to finish your prototype, release your beta, and get that precious feedback you need to rapidly iterate and tweak your product. Also, the more you focus, the less chance there is of colliding with a competitor. Start dead simple, measure your feedback, and learn from it," is the advice given by startup co-founders Brian Erke and Ryan Halper.

In summary

So far, we have reviewed the following laws for great decision-making:

> *Law #1: Know your drive for decision-making*
> *Law #2: Clearly define the challenge you are trying to solve*
> *Law #3: Focus on adding value and delivering clear benefits*
> *Law #4: Limit the risk of your decisions*

By applying the above framework to your decision-making process you will start with a coherent set of reasons and goals for being in business, you will clearly describe one specific business challenge you are addressing, you will be committed to delivering distinctive benefits to your stakeholders and you will keep your risks low by conducting small, controlled experiments.

A couple of decades of experience in business has taught me that following the *opposite* approach may lead to great decision-making only by *pure chance!* While disaster is not guaranteed, you are more likely to waste your time and put your resources at risk when making decisions haphazardly. I know so because I have experienced it. The ups and downs have taught me to conduct business in a more logical and focused manner, building like a social weaver bird, starting small, improving, then expanding.

In the following chapters, we will dive deeper into these concepts to continue building a company that key stakeholders and investors find attractive.

- CHAPTER 5 -

Guide the superstars

Multiply your ability to make great decisions

"No one can whistle a symphony. It takes an orchestra to play it."–H.E. Luccock

Perhaps one of sports greatest teams of all time was the Brazil 1970 soccer team that went on to win the World Cup, with a star-studded squad featuring Pelé. Their head coach, Mario Zagallo, became a true icon of the Brazilian game, winning two World Cups as a player in 1958 and 1962, one as a national manager in 1970 and his final one as assistant manager in 1994.

Despite the fantastic array of players that Zagallo had at his disposal, it was ultimately up to him to mould all the star material into a cohesive unit truly working together as a team. Many in Brazil, were uncertain if Pelé and Tostao would be able to play beside each other, but in the end, Zagallo proved it was possible thanks to his system and his leadership allowing individuals to shine within the structure of a well-conceived game plan. This resulted in a play that was "both efficient and pleasing to the eye, from the dribbling and powerful strikes to explosive runs, drives out of midfield to the unparalleled inspiration of Pelé himself", according to FIFA accounts.

While it could be argued that the level of play of individual players would have been sufficient to pull off a World Cup win, bad leadership could have also brought down the Brazil squad. In the end, Zagallo's approach created the synergy necessary to win at the highest competitive level.

Likewise, in business, companies aim to hire the best talent they can afford, but as we will see, recruiting the best is only the start. Great decision-making calls for putting together a particular type of team that multiplies the company's ability to make great decisions.

LAW #5:

MULTIPLY YOUR ABILITY TO MAKE GREAT DECISIONS WITH HPTS

Why Law #5?

If you are left to make great decisions by yourself, you will quickly find out it is an exhausting process that can drain your ability to make great decisions.

Great decision making is strengthened when decision-makers share values and a common results-driven framework with team members in special teams known as high-performance teams (HPTs).

The HPT approach aims to create synergies that will make decision-making more powerful by embedding it into enterprise culture and multiplying the firm's capacity to make great decisions.

The lack of HPT culture and practice may result in an over-reliance on management to make every decision and solve every problem, slowing value creation for stakeholders.

Maximising results: high-performance teams

In my early years as an entrepreneur, I learned that you could only do so much before you burnout or before you fail due to lack of traction—and trying to do it all by yourself is not the answer. I knew I needed a better framework for delivering results; a sustainable one that did not depend on me to make every single decision and one that would unlock the team's potential. That's where I came across high-performance teams.

A team can be defined as an interdependent group of individuals who share responsibility and a common goal. A *high-performance team* (HPT) on the other hand is not only an interdependent, but *stable, role-defined*, group of individuals who share responsibility as well as *mutual trust*, and *values*, while having *strong leadership*, clear *focus* and a common goal.

Robin Bard defines a high-performance team as a group of people with specific roles and complementary talents and skills, aligned with and committed to a common purpose, who consistently exhibit high levels of collaboration and innovation, produce superior results. The high-performance team is regarded as a tightly-knit unit, focused on their goal and have supportive processes that will enable team members to overcome barriers in the achievement of their collective goals.

Pat MacMillan of Triaxia Partners posits that a HPT team model must be focused on achieving business results. It starts with a common purpose, clear roles underpinned by interdependence, accepted leadership, effective processes, stable relationships, excellent communication, all of which is driven by cooperation.

According to the Triaxia HPT model, business results are at the centre of focus, under the assumption that a contributor cannot achieve them single-handedly—the whole point of collaborating is precisely to achieve what you cannot do by yourself in a more efficient way.

Again, it is highlighted that the point of HPTs is to deliver *value* to stakeholders; that is, the decision-maker is centred on delivering *results*.

HPTs starts with recruitment

The assembly of high-performance teams starts with methodical recruitment. Throughout my years in business, I have gone searching around the world for talented contributors who could help us build a great company. I looked for professionals who were not only technically gifted but also able to collaborate and work as team players. I have also been fortunate to find great people who decided to join.

From my experience of starting, building and selling my company, I became an expert at recruiting. Having a clear idea of who your "A-Team" should be is central to building a great company that solves your users' problems. The exact mix of talent that you require will depend on your unique set of circumstances, but ultimately it is this mix that helps determine your startup's trajectory.

Only hire for roles where you know exactly what the tasks are, how that individual will be valued, and what a great job looks like. If you do need to hire, then be sure, to be honest about what you don't know and bring on people that have that experience.

Interviewing and hiring are skills that must be learned and practised. Don't wing it and then expect good results. Bring in mentors and advisors into the interview process to teach you how to hire.

As a decision-maker, I keep reminding myself to find people who complement the team's skills, resisting the urge to hire people who are too alike to me or to current members. To build a high-performance team, the decision-maker will hire to close out the skills gap, to strengthen the team in weak areas.

The other aspect to remember is that a fundamental need is for each member to establish themselves as individuals while also having a strong sense of belonging to the team. If this healthy tension can be maintained and nurtured, the result will likely be a stronger team able to make great decisions.

In your planning, ensure that roles are well defined, compatible, complementary and delegated based on the strength of each member's skills. This configuration will lead to natural synergies.

As I was building the team, one of the approaches I took was to start small and progressively increase the level of challenges both in technical and managerial complexity. By this, I mean giving increased overall responsibility. Another essential thing to look for is the initiative: does the employee proactively contribute and solve problems for the company without being nudged continuously?

Forget what worked previously

You just cannot build a company from the ground up without high calibre people. It is inspiring to work with professionals who have solved problems and continue to add value to our clients on a daily basis. As a company grows from one stage to the next, you have to throw out what worked and change your mindset to the next mode for success.

For the early team, optimise for the ability to get things done, not any specific experience. Very few people can actually push a task over the finish line. But, once you hit initial traction, you have to switch to optimizing for hiring people who can build systems. Through that transition, adding bodies without systems and processes only creates more chaos.

Powerful goals will help keep you focused

After much trial and error, I also learned about the power of goal setting. According to HPT theory, the most effective goals are clear, relevant, significant, urgent, and achievable. A great example of this singular goal focus is seen in sports, and it is one of the reasons for their appeal. When you are a player on the field there is little doubt as to what you are supposed to achieve; whether it is scoring a point or arriving first in the race, you know exactly what you are there for. When this is translated to a business context it has a powerful effect on results and on team dynamics. On the contrary, When this kind of goal definition is lacking it is easy for the team to get distracted with many other concerns.

One way to ensure that the team stays focused on the goal is to keep the lines of communication open at all times. Distractions can and will come from multiple angles, including personal, family, on top of business-related issues. If the goal is kept visible it will be easier to re-focus on the ultimate aim of the team. Be open about the state of affairs and on your progress en route to your shared goal.

Building trust

The lack of trust in a team slows everything down or makes it impossible to achieve results altogether. Hence, underpinning all other efforts is the trust built across the team but especially the trust placed on leadership. Leadership consultant Joseph Folkman points out three basic pillars upon which trust is built relationships, expertise and consistency. Folkman posits that healthy relationships ought to be developed across the team and company-wide, that knowledge or expertise must be established, leading to confidence being placed on the member and finally, consistency, ensuring that promises are kept and that others know what to expect.

In *The Captain Class*, author Sam Walker adds another dimension to the above, pointing out the qualities of elite captains. These include competitiveness, willingness to perform thankless jobs in the shadows, a low-key, practical communication style and the ability to motivate others with non-verbal displays. Walker also highlights the importance of strong conviction and of having ironclad emotional control.

From years of my experience, I can relate to the importance of building and maintaining the fabric of trust. This confidence in each other can be slow to develop, but it is one of the most precious assets of any team. Nurture it and guard it as it can be a fragile asset.

Conflict management

Given the variety of personalities, backgrounds, and styles, differences of opinion are likely to emerge at some point. Misunderstandings and open conflict are to be expected as part of team dynamics. The difference between regular teams and HPTs is being prepared with clear, established procedures for dealing with and solving swiftly is the preferred approach for HPTs. Management must not assume that conflicts will always resolve itself independently and have clear guidelines instead.

However, if no proper conflict resolution guidelines are provided, egos can flare up, conflict can undermine the fabric of trust and wreak unnecessary havoc in the HPT.

Along with proper guidelines, the key skill for HPTs to develop is the ability to spot and address interpersonal issues promptly. This is crucial because otherwise the capacity of the team to make decisions can be severely undermined, so that focus on the goal is restored. Unresolved issues can be costly not only in terms of personal and professional relationships but ultimately in the lack of business results.

Key inner-team relationships

One of the essential pieces of advice I learned: never undervalue the relationship you have with your cofounders, your significant other, or their significant others. You'll ultimately spend more time with your cofounders on a daily basis. Knowing your cofounder plans and ambitions and life situation, as well as their significant other's, and whether they align with yours over a long horizon, really matter. It's impossible in many cases to overcome incompatibility. Talk about this early, often, and make time for regular updates.

Some things to think about: can you survive three months at a time apart? Can you move if the business requires it? How will workloads impact family planning? What kind of outcome are we looking for from the business? How long can it take for us to get there? There are no wrong answers to any of these questions, so long as everyone is on the same page.

Don't enter into relationships adversarially. It's effortless to think in us versus them terms of investors, partners, and even co-founders. One of the most sincerely toxic things I've seen in startups is ultimately shortsighted thinking: investor X is useless, I shouldn't have taken their money, they're not letting me do what I want to do. Even if all of those things are true, play the long game, our careers are lengthier than our startups, and when you entered into the relationship, you gained something. Spend as much emotional time as you can thinking about the perspectives of everyone around you, plan for the outcomes and concerns they might have, and maintain good relationships. When you start thinking in terms of us – our investment team, etc. you've won.

The employee right-decision test

To help me make better decisions regarding employee evaluation and suitability, I came up with "employee right-decision test" consisting of two parts. First, I would ask myself: "If employee x handed in their notice, would I be upset and fight to keep them?"

Secondly, I would question if I could go back in time, would I offer them the job again. If the answer to both of these questions is yes, you have made a great decision in hiring that employee. Otherwise, that employee is not the right fit for your business and you need to find a person that you would answer *yes* for.

The first employee I had to let go was a very stressful experience from a personal perspective. Separating the emotional from the business component is not an easy process, so as a manager you go through a variety of emotions and run endless scenarios in your head. However, once you see the business relationship through the lens of the performance criteria it is much easier to make an objective decision.

It is crucial to develop a common framework for evaluating performance that both manager and employee share. This way, the fit can be evaluated in an objective (and less emotional) way. With some luck and tact, employees will realise that they are not right for the roles.

As a founder, hiring and firing are the only two jobs; you'll have from founding to exit as a constant. Being bad at either leads to suboptimal outcomes. Embrace the process for both because after being at the helm for a few years, you'll have done both hundreds of times. They're both equally difficult to master (and both can save your business at the critical time). "Hire slowly and fire quickly," suggests Amitav Chakravartty of VaycayHero.

If you are firing people correctly, it will not be a surprise to them. The wrong way is to fire someone and not accurately gather evidence as to why the person should be fired. To precisely document performance, make sure to set expectations clear by giving clear warnings, and you and the employee should track progress through time task keeping and weekly (or maybe daily tasks, if you're in a rush to fire) to-do lists.

Setting clear expectations

Setting clear expectations helps employees see what they need to change and if they are making those changes or not. If they are not rising to the challenge, they know it and are not surprised if it ends with them moving on.

It is very rare that an average employee will step up the game and become stellar. Meanwhile, a lot of the CEO's and team's time is spent trying to improve underperforming employee's performance.

Hence, an average/underperforming employee not only costs money but also imposes severe morale and time-spent tax on a young company. The faster you let go, the faster you will bring in a materially better person who will do the job well.

HPTs in theory and in practice

In retrospect, I see that as time passed, my ideas on how to run a company coupled with feedback and experience became practice. The test of time made the best practices in terms of how our business would be run. For me, the key insight was that I needed to take the time to *reflect* on how we got things done and not just accept or assume our practice had to be the *best*.

I wondered if there was a better approach to achieving results that optimised the combined talent we had hired and which could guide recruitment going forward? But it is often the case that management theory sounds appealing and inspiring, but in practice, it becomes messy or impossible to implement without significant detours or without major adaptations. And as I have learned, HPT theory is no exception—it must be adapted to suit your reality and particular needs, depending on the stage of your company.

I reminded myself that regardless of the hiring budget teams will have differences of opinion and there will be conflict, but the point is to take it into account and plan for it so that you are not only able to deal with it effectively but to capitalise and even thrive on it.

Tuckman's stages of team development (forming, storming, norming, performing, adjourning) are a useful reminder of the different challenges teams will face, and that effectiveness will vary depending on the stage you are in. Early on behaviour is cautious as everyone is getting acquainted, but tensions start to arise as members establish their positions. Then—if you have the right framework in place—conflicts are resolved, and members appreciate each other's strengths. If this trend continues the team becomes increasingly cohesive, and less input is needed from the leader.

Building a high-performance team centred on powerful goals, multiplies your capacity to make great decisions.

- CHAPTER 6 -

Design your water slides

Empower others to automate decision-making

"Leaders don't create followers; they create more leaders." —Tom Peters

Rick Hunter is president and CEO of ProSlide Technology, a company which has designed some of the world's most impressive water slides. Applying physics principles, ProSlide designs builds and tests how the human body reacts to the twists and turns of these thrill-inducing waterpark attractions. One of the challenges they have successfully solved over the years is allowing riders of all sizes and weights to negotiate the twists and turns at about the same speed. He explains that to solve it you control the flow of water—with the right volume and flow speed heavier riders will move at the speed of the water and likewise, lighter rides will be flushed and pushed forward. The result is that regardless of the weight, riders tend to reach a similar speed. This, however, does not apply for straight and steep drops, where heavy riders do come out faster than lighter ones. In that case, riders are cleared to go only once the last person is out.

Water slide complexity

ProSlide is innovators who have successfully deployed serpentine rides, twin-entry loading bays, kids-only rides, 6-person slides and U-shaped flumes. They also invented the first hybrid ride with multiple bowl features and the 6-person water coaster ride. Lastly, the braided mat racer allows for 6 or more riders to race each other side by side. With an increasing number of elements and layouts they can render highly intricate flow designs that include slides and tunnels resulting in an almost infinite amount of combinations. ProSlide also designs the more traditional straight-forward drops being ultimately up to the customers to decide the specific configuration that best suits their waterpark.

The water slide analogy: *flow rules*

Once your business has reached a particular stage of maturity, and your HPTs are operating at full speed, the number of decisions may increase. It is very tempting for the decision-maker, especially the founders and senior business leaders to attempt to monopolise decision-making. However, not all decisions are created equal, and some can be automated to a certain extent, especially those that are repetitive. Without such systems and frameworks in place, you would end up micro-managing, probably exhausting yourself and limiting organisational growth.

The water slide analogy hints at the need for a structure that informs the decision-making process, leading to a certain degree of automation. In this scenario, imagine that a rider at the top of the slide represents a decision that needs to be made and the water slides represent the rules on how to handle that decision, telling the rider how to navigate the system to achieve a desirable outcome for all. Without the careful arrangement of slides, the rider would not end up being thrilled and ecstatic at the end of the process, that is, the decision would not be made correctly, and every single decision would have to be consulted with the owner—hardly a scalable company. But if done correctly, your flow rules will empower you and your organisation to make great decisions and reduce the burden of repetitive decision-making.

LAW #6:

AUTOMATE YOUR SYSTEMS & FRAMEWORKS FOR REPETITIVE DECISION-MAKING

Why Law #6?

The design of frameworks will allow you to approach decision-making more systematically.

Your ability to make great decisions is enhanced if you are able to focus on the *exceptions*—on the choices that do require your input, leaving the repetitive ones to be handled by your framework, empowering teams to manage such decisions.

Moreover, frameworks can also help you automate the way you work with your teams so that there is a natural flow of inputs and outputs.

The thoughtful design of these systems will increase your overall capacity to make great decisions.

On the contrary, a lack of these systems may result in an over-reliance on management to make every decision and solve every problem, slowing value creation for stakeholders.

Automate to scale

As a decision-maker, you aim to grow and expand as much as you can with your value-creation machine, that is, your organisation and its ability to serve customers. To do so create systems to replicate and automate the delivery with a focus on efficient use of resources. Value creation is optimised when you generate the most amount of value with the least amount of resources.

One approach I liked was referenced by Brian Chesky, Airbnb founder, where entrepreneurs were encouraged to do things that *don't* scale, that is, to start with the ideal mix of benefits for users, one at a time, then finding ways to replicate that ten times, one hundred times, a thousand times and so on. It is about getting it right the first time, not necessarily asking if it scales from Day 1. We did that before bringing in the systems to scale operations.

It is very evident to see that customers (and investors) reward companies that can scale their value creation processes—it is one of the main reasons that data-driven and algorithm-driven companies will continue to thrive.

Empowering great decision-making

Micro-management is the opposite of great decision-making. It slows down your decision-making process and prevents your HPT members from growing and gaining ownership of their ideas and execution. The micro-manager sends the message that only what he or she does and approves is the right way of doing things, but in the process also becomes the single point of failure for their department or the company as a whole. In contrast, the great decision-maker realises that a better alternative is to *empower others* to make great decisions.

However, in my experience, the journey to empowerment is not a straightforward one. It can be challenging for members to determine if they have gone too far, making a decision or if they are too timid. To counter this, one of the approaches has been to create rules or *boundaries* that empower team members and simplify management.

One example of this was when I informed my team that they had the discretion to resolve customer issues up to a certain budget depending on specific criteria. In other words, they were free to make their own call as long as it didn't go beyond the agreed threshold. In practical terms, it meant they could dedicate company resources that didn't go over the budget. The staff instantly gained a sense of ownership as stewards of company resources, knowing they could not be faulted for a decision they made within the agreed boundaries. I found it made everyone feel more trustworthy and proactive, it resulted in happier customers, *and* it freed up my own time.

Payoffs vs risk decision-making frameworks

The more comprehensive approach to this is to develop a larger framework for decision-making. I imagine it not unlike the network of slides and tunnels created by ProSlide, reading like a diagram of how riders flow from A to B or from J to K, with a level of complexity according to the business needs.

A decision framework should guide HPT members to make their own decisions within the confines of agreed boundaries, whether it is simple binary conditions or more complex rules and guidelines, but always empowered with certain levels of discretion.

It is based on the basic principle of payoffs vs risk. If you trust that a particular decision-making process will result in a potentially good payoff for the company and the risk is relatively low, then the team or member is free to pursue it without further need to rely on management.

But based on the same approach, if the decision involves a high level of risk for the company, then a decision is unjustified, and the conversation must be taken back to management.

Your framework could map out like a matrix with gradients of *payoffs vs risk* in low, medium and high areas so that it is more evident for all to see what is encouraged and what is off-limits.

It also helps to write down such a framework based on your own experience running the company. In other words, after you have done it yourself, you can have a better idea of what works and what doesn't, while being open to finding new ways of optimising decision-making and value creation.

The overall benefit of your decision-making frameworks is to instil more autonomy in your teams within certain boundaries of risk.

A study of 320 companies by Cornell University concluded that companies that give employees decision-making autonomy tend to grow four times faster and experience a third of the turnover of those companies run with more conventional top-down management structures.

With that said, remember that mistakes will happen and risks will be incurred in. However, these are the expected associated costs of great decision-making. Keep in mind the alternative is more expensive and quite unsustainable: making every single little decision yourself.

Objectives and Key Results (OKRs)

A related type of challenge that I have faced in my journey was being able to agree on a system for goal setting. Without shared goals, it becomes challenging for others to see how their work fits in the grand scheme of things. While management theory provides a wide range of frameworks and approaches for setting organisational and individual goals, I needed a lightweight system for achieving it; I came across Objectives and Key Results (OKR) management system. It proved to be a system that everyone in the business could use; everyone, including myself and board members, used the system to achieve unifying objectives. This created a culture of togetherness and collaboration and removed traditional reporting boundaries, creating a common framework for making great decisions regarding our own goals and objectives.

Objectives and Key Results

Objectives and Key Results (OKR) is a framework for defining and tracking objectives and their outcomes.

OKRs comprise an objective, a clearly defined goal, and one or more key results or specific measures used to track the achievement of that goal. The development of OKRs is generally attributed to Intel co-founder and CEO Andy Grove. The key result must be measurable. More recently, OKRs became central to Google's culture as a "management methodology that helps to ensure that the company focuses efforts on the same important issues throughout the organisation." Larry Page, the CEO of Alphabet and co-founder of Google, explains that "OKRs have helped lead us to 10x growth, many times over. They've helped make our crazily bold mission of 'organising the world's information' perhaps even achievable." Today OKRs are prevalent in several tech companies.

Objectives and Key Results help everyone focus on what is most relevant to the company in the current stage. When each person understands how their individual OKRs contribute to the company's overall OKRs, it is much easier to appreciate everyone's work. This leads to a more supportive work environment where each person helps the other achieve their objectives. Collaboration becomes a by-product of this simple but powerful management system.

Boundaries can free you up to make great decisions

As a decision-maker, one of your most precious assets is time—time to reflect on your priorities, your strategy, your resources and opportunities. The ability of the great decision-maker to see the big picture and *not* get lost in the details is a fundamental one that may determine if you make or break the company.

Setting up your organisation with systems and frameworks for great decision-making will free your time to help you focus on the long-term vision and the opportunities that may not be so obvious at first sight. But if you're caught up with day to day trivial decision-making will be hard to keep making the great decisions that matter in a sustainable way.

Just like the water slides that allow riders to extract great joy from experience, the slides are also boundaries that limit riders' exposure to risk.

By giving careful thought to the design of the *water slides* for your own company, you will likely increase the value (and fun) for your stakeholders while limiting your overall risk.

- CHAPTER 7 -

Time your swing

Deciding means taking action at the right time

"In any moment of decision, the best thing you can do is the right thing, the next best thing is the wrong thing, and the worst thing you can do is nothing."–Theodore Roosevelt

One of the hardest feats in the world of professional sports is hitting off a Major League Baseball pitcher hurling a ball at over 90 miles per hour (145 kilometres per hour) from a distance of just over 18 metres from you. It takes less than half a second for the baseball to reach the batter, from the time the ball is released from the pitcher's hand to the point of contact with the bat. To the untrained eye, the fastball is but a quick blur.

On August 13, 2017, at Yankee Stadium in New York City, Rafael Devers of the Boston Red Sox walked up to the batter's box to face superstar relief pitcher Aroldis Chapman. The clue as to how fast Chapman can throw a baseball is in his nickname: the *Cuban Missile* or the *Cuban Flame Thrower*. While an average professional baseball pitcher can throw a fastball somewhere above the 90-mph mark, Chapman's fastball is consistently clocked at around 100-mph (161-kph). As of 2019, Chapman holds the Guinness

World Record for the fastest pitch ever thrown with a speed of just over 105-mph.

With his team trailing by just one run in the last inning of play, Rafael Devers would be fortunate to put the ball in play against the *Cuban Flame Thrower*. On the fourth pitch, Devers made history on a pitch clocked at just under 103-mph—he hit a game-tying home run. Devers hit "the hardest pitch any player has homered off since Major League Baseball started officially tracking pitch velocity in 2008". Some have called it the impossible homerun.

To understand the difficulty of this accomplishment, we must consider that light from the ball as it is released by the pitcher reaches the eye instantly. However, it takes the brain about 50 milliseconds (ms) to actually *see* the ball. Then the hitter has about 150 ms to process the image, *decide* to swing or not and start to contract the muscles to actually move the bat across the plate.

Hovering through space as it nears the hitter, the baseball has a limited window of opportunity where it can be successfully hit. To hit a home run several very precise movements must be coordinated: the swing must be timed perfectly so that the ball is hit squarely, the bat must be positioned at the right angle in relation to the centre of the ball, and the bat needs to move with enough momentum (bat speed). If done right, the ball's trajectory will clear the outfield fence for a home run, and it all must be orchestrated within a split second. But if the batter swings too early or too late the ball could be missed altogether.

Window of opportunity

We have so far established the following logical flow for great decision-making:

> *Law #1: Know your drive for decision-making*
> *Law #2: Clearly define the challenge you are trying to solve*
> *Law #3: Focus on adding value and delivering clear benefits*
> *Law #4: Limit the risk of your decisions*
> *Law #5: Multiply your ability to make great decisions with high-performance teams*
> *Law #6: Automate your systems and frameworks for repetitive decision-making*

The above approach makes it easier to make great decisions, including those to free up your time and to multiply your ability to make great decisions. But at the end of the day, it is the job of the decision-maker to actually *make decisions*. And just like the ball approaching the hitter, decisions have a shelf life—they must be made within their window of opportunity. It is important for the decision-maker to realise in advance that many times the perfect decision will not exist, but that a decision must be made nevertheless.

LAW #7:

DECIDE IN A TIMELY MANNER

Why Law #7?

The value that a great decision-maker adds to their organisations is the ability to actually make decisions when the time comes. Simply put, once all has been considered, the decision-maker must make a decision.

Your teams and frameworks can handle much of the day-to-day decision-making, but companies grow by solving problems and seizing opportunities when decisions are made at the right time.

The alternative is deciding too early or too late, or not at all, creating unnecessary burdens for the organisation.

Deciding in a timely manner is associated with seasoned managers and senior business leaders who recognise that making the right decision can be as important as choosing on time, even if the *perfect* decision is not made.

Management by Exception

In Chapter 6, we established that it is useful to automate the organisation with systems and frameworks for great repetitive decision-making. If done well, perhaps four out of five decisions might be handled by our systems with minimal to no input from the key decision-maker. As the system is perfected, the frameworks make operations more seamless, and a decreasing number of every-day decisions need to be handled by the key decision-maker, freeing up time to strategise and innovate. Our focus here is on the *exceptions*, on the decisions that *must* be controlled by the decision-maker, those that cannot and should not be delegated.

Paralysis by analysis

Overanalysing or overthinking an issue in the search for the perfect decision can be an easy trap to fall into. As a decision-maker, you are expected to keep a cool head in the midst of chaos. And more often than not, it will be incredibly useful to delay making a decision as long as possible to give you time to go over the facts and ensure that you are not reacting from gut instinct.

This can be a true sign of wisdom, but if overdone, it can also backfire when decision-making becomes paralysed by an indefinite need for information or for a seemingly indefinite time to process. Especially if a situation seems too complex or overwhelming, a decision may never be made, out of fear of causing greater problems.

This state of *suppressed decision-making* may also be an effort to keep options open, but it can lead to the same result of indecision. And if the decision-maker is unable to provide an answer when it is due, it may trigger a chain of consequences that come with greater risks than having made a relatively wrong decision in the first place. This can include loss of confidence in the manager's ability to lead. On the contrary, impulsiveness in decision-making can also damage trust, so the decision-maker must be aware of not swinging the bat too early either.

Decidere: cutting off what you will not pursue

In my quest to become a better decision-maker, I searched the word root for "decision" and "to decide". I found that the root word *cis* and its variants *cid* and *cide* come from a Latin root *decidere* which means 'cut' or 'kill.' A decision made implies 'cutting off' of all possibilities except for one; if you are decisive you 'kill' other options. This is not an easy thing to do.

While the idea of saying no to alternatives may sound limiting, in my experience, I have found that it is quite the opposite: it is liberating to commit to a course of action—you declare your choice, and you free your company to pursue that chosen option.

The key distinction I made is that deciding is knowing what you *will not do*. In a sense, this is easier because, by a process of elimination, you figure out what does *not* work before opting for a given path.

The alternative is dragging along for the ride all the possible choices with the difficulty of consuming your precious mental space and potentially company resources. Just like a closet full of unworn clothes or an endless inventory of useless spares—it is wise to only keep at hand what you will require within reason.

Saying no

In business we are typically great at taking on more work, at saying *yes* to customers and sales, that's what we're here for, right? But doing so mindlessly can come at the price of people's time and company resources.

In our case, we had invested significantly in the development of our own cloud collaboration service, and it was selling in high numbers, we were all high-fiving ourselves. Like a rocket out of nowhere, Microsoft launched into the market their own collaboration solution with a vastly superior offering in every way; overall it represented a better solution and outcomes for our customers. Our sales team wanted to sell both solutions, and the path of least resistance was indeed to sell both. However, I decided to focus all our efforts (technical, sales, marketing) on the Microsoft solutions and cut out our own . This gave our customers a superior solution while simplifying the use of resources utilised in sales and deployment. It took away what would have been a distraction at that point unifying efforts around a focused offering.

Committing to a course of action

Deciding in a timely manner is perhaps one of the most complex functions of the decision-maker because, in many ways, it is a decision that must ultimately be made by a single person or a very small team. In an ideal scenario, the decision is brought to your attention when your frameworks cannot handle it. You come to this point after discussions, consultations and your own research. After considering all the facts and calmly reflecting on all the options you are then left by yourself to conclude, to kill unfeasible options and choose the one that makes the most sense. But all of this must be done while the window of opportunity is still open—you must swing your bat when it is time to do so, not whenever it might suit your own needs.

Embrace making *wrong* decisions

And to get to that seemingly *enlightened* state of great decision-making, you must be comfortable with making *wrong* decisions. Throughout my years of making good and bad decisions, I have learned that there is only one way to make great decisions and that is *making* them.

You won't be able to pull the trigger if you don't accept that at times you will get it wrong, that you will not be perfect and that you will have to deal with the consequences of all decision-making. This includes decisions that go well but also those that do not work for you and your company. The alternative is postponing, expecting committees to decide, or indefinitely putting off a decision. Sometimes the price of inaction can be so damaging that it cannot be rationally justified. And what happens when you make the wrong decision? The answer is that you learn and you move on.

In my experience, making a decision when it is time to do so builds trust and improves your ability to make great decisions in the long run.

- CHAPTER 8 –

Check your blind spots

Beware of your assumptions

"The fool wonders, the wise man asks." –
Benjamin Disraeli

Imagine the following scenario which could have been recorded as dashcam video evidence in a major motorway anywhere around the world: a car has just exited the motorway and joined six-lane traffic, staying in the far left lane. Fast approaching from its right is a heavy goods vehicle—the truck driver is attempting to merge to the far left; however it misses a small detail: the car that is already travelling on that lane. It does not seem to notice it and proceeds to merge, resulting in the car being pushed towards the hard shoulder. The car eventually spins around towards the front of the truck and narrowly avoids further damage. This time both vehicles had a lucky escape.

Vehicle blind spots

Vehicle blind spots—areas where the driver cannot see while looking ahead or through mirrors—are about the size of a large swimming pool but much more substantial for a larger vehicle. However, trucks have a larger number of invisible areas as compared to other passenger vehicles. According to the National Highway

Traffic Safety Administration, each year over 800 thousand accidents related to blind spots occur each year in the US alone. This is partly due to drivers not adjusting their mirrors properly, or not adequately checking blind spots before changing lanes.

Blind Spot Warning Systems

To counter this, blind spot detection was first introduced by car manufacturers in 2007, producing a visible alert while switching lanes and attempting to move into a blind spot area by using two door-mounted cameras monitoring for possible collisions.

In the past decade, detection has evolved through the use of short-range radar sensors scanning areas directly alongside and behind the car. In addition to cameras and radar technology, blind-spot warning systems may also include ultrasonic sensors alongside the car, spotting vehicles that may otherwise go undetected by the driver. Increasingly sophisticated blind-spot warning systems help drivers steer away from unsafe merging or lane-changing, preventing countless blind spot accidents, helping them safely reach their destination.

Blind spots in decision-making

Likewise, decision-makers aim to reach their goals as efficiently and safely as possible. While confidence in decision-making is a desired attribute, overconfidence in one's own ability to make decisions can also lead to poor judgment in decision-making when warning signals and potential obstacles are ignored. "We're generally overconfident in our opinions and our impressions and our judgments. We exaggerate how knowable the world is" cautions psychologist and economist Daniel Kahneman.

Organisational behavioural expert, Dr Loretta Malandro, explains that decision-makers can be confronted with several decision-making blind spots. These include the "I know" attitude, where one's opinion should be the best or most valued one. The underlying assumption here is that we—at the helm of, or in a key position in the company—have the best visibility of all that we need to consider for making a great decision. However, for a variety of reasons, this may not always be the case.

LAW #8:

ASK FOR EXPERT ADVICE

Why Law #8?

Despite the great amount of reflection that a decision-maker can give to any particular situation, some circumstances may turn out to be more complex than anticipated or inadequate for the decision-makers frameworks and systems to handle.

In such cases, a great decision may be reached by consulting experts with a proven track record or advisors who can provide useful perspectives not previously considered.

Expert advice may help cast light on decision-making blind spots which were not previously seen by the decision-maker leading to significant improvements in the quality of decision-making. In some cases, asking for advice may not only result in marginal improvement but can also help avoid significant pitfalls.

There's no need to go at it alone

In my path to become a better decision-maker, I analysed the process by which I made decisions, such as the quality of information I had available, the voices that influenced my decisions and the rationale behind a decision at a particular time.

I had turned the focus inwards, from looking at the company only, to the mechanism by which I made decisions as part of the company. In doing so, I was able to improve my decision-making success and remove influences that were not adding value to decision-making.

But when faced with problems—and as a founder or business leader, you'll face many—I was tempted to solve them my own way, reinventing the proverbial wheel more than once. But why do so when any given problem has already been solved by someone else?

Do you opt then to start from scratch or get help? The former can be incredibly time-consuming and expensive; trying to solve a problem by building something from scratch, when the solution is already out there, in the form of advice, a product or service is a form of wasted resources. Depending on your particular situation, asking for help can be a much more efficient approach.

And while decision-making oftentimes feel like a lonely endeavour, I quickly realised that there was no need for me to go at it alone—I started calling for help.

Distinguish advice from opinion

First off, a key lesson I learned in making great decisions is to understand the difference between advice and opinion. I learned that advice is offered by someone who has experience and has walked the talk, whereas opinion is a belief, a guess, a subjective view.

Advice is based on knowledge or experience within a specific domain gained by doing or by conducting research. On the other hand, an opinion is based on what someone *thinks*, not what they necessarily know. It is crucial to develop the ability to distinguish the difference. It is up to you, the decision-maker to tell opinion apart from advice so that you can make a fair evaluation and come to your own conclusion. The success of your business may hinge on the ability to discern between opinion and expert advice.

Dealing with conflicting advice

Once you ask you will probably receive loads of advice (or opinions). What may have worked for someone else may not really work for you. To complicate matters, you may receive advice that sounds right but completely contradicts what someone else has said to you. In this scenario, it is always important to take a step back to understand the reasons for that advice.

Critical thinking on the part of the founder is a key skill that is often implied but typically overlooked. You may want to look at the motivations behind any particular piece of advice and also the limitations from that particular source. It is in no way meant to disqualify potentially helpful advice, but it is important to understand the point of the view of that source. One of the questions I asked myself when listening to advice is: is this person an expert in the field? Have they done this? Assessing if that person has the experience lends more authority to any word of advice and helps deal with conflicting pieces of advice.

Tap into experts with a proven record

Mentor networks and other professional support groups specialised in helping startups can be incredibly helpful to ramp up your chances of success. I was fortunate to have access to current and retired tech industry executives who readily engaged with us from early on.

If you don't know where to get help lookup mentor support networks in your area. You're almost guaranteed to find one within close range. If not geographically close to you, there is an increasing number of networks available online.

You can look for advice on a number of general and specialised networks with varying degrees of formality. As I previously said, always rely on your critical thinking skills to qualify what is being recommended and ask the necessary questions.

Identify your blindspots and tap the shoulder of those who have done it. I've done this every step of the way, and it has made a difference, challenging me to think better and to focus on solving the problems that matter. Sometimes the advice can be painful, so be prepared to act accordingly once you are clear on it.

Board of Advisors

After we had reached a significant level of sales, I wanted to take it to the next level—I knew I needed a board, but I had no previous experience in assembling one. I was resolved to tap on experienced business people who could help me fast track the business and shortcut mistakes. I understood that setting up a board was an important step signalling that I was serious about scaling the company. I had to consider the advantages and disadvantages of running a board.

There is a crucial difference between a board of directors and a board of advisors. From a legal perspective, advisors have no legal obligations, and they have no voting rights. Advisors offer advice to directors who are not compelled to implement the advice. A board of advisors serves more like a sounding board, leaving it up to the executive team to follow recommendations.

On the other hand, the board of Directors membership comes with legal responsibilities as well as voting rights. Moreover, the executive team is required to carry out the resolutions of the board of Directors. Technically it is important to remember that once you form a corporation, you automatically have a board of Directors. The board of Directors is ultimately responsible and liable for the company's actions.

Benefits of a Board

A great board will be enriched with a variety of backgrounds, talent and specific know-how. The diversity in this mix will help you avoid groupthink which can lead to poor decision-making and is a known trap that may kill innovation and growth. Typically, a board will include industry experts, marketing or sales as well as financial specialists.

Moreover, the board helps avoid strategic or tactical mistakes that executives can make on their own. Not being in the daily grind of operations enables members to see a broader view of the field and with the benefit of experience, this can translate to wiser decisions for your company.

The other important aspect of boards is the access they provide to key stakeholders, including potential customers and business partners. Well connected board members can make highly valuable introductions that could translate to contracts and/or key partnerships. Moreover, these contacts can solve specific problems that may arise in day-to-day business. However, as a CEO you must be careful not to overdo it by constantly requesting help from the board. Preferably you would like a board member to *offer* to make an introduction as opposed to you asking for it.

The third aspect which I think is an essential benefit is the level of legitimacy and trust that a functioning board lends to the company. The stature and respect that your board members have earned over the years translate into trust in the eyes of key stakeholders such as investors. The flipside of this is if your members are too famous, they may have little time to take your calls (or for board meetings). Ideally, you want to strike a balance between the level of eminence and approachability. It is OK to ask how much time they could devote to your company. It is up to you to decide if you want a hands-on, approachable board member or more of a letterhead-only board member who is not actively engaged in your business but who could open doors.

I chose to form a strong, active board for all of the above reasons. I understood that it could take months and years off my learning curve. Indeed the overall effect was to cast light on decision-making blind spots making me more confident in my ability to make great decisions.

Talk to great decision-makers

In addition to forming a board, it is a great idea for decision-makers to talk to people you consider great decision-makers, including specialists in key areas. I learned over the years to talk to people with an open mind, not looking for validation for a decision that I already had made; there is nothing more formative than flexing your critical thinking skills by listening to experts with opposing viewpoints. The tension in the difference of opinions is an invitation to explore new ideas and to keep learning about different alternatives. This is especially important when major strategic paths are being considered or when decisions of major consequence are to be taken.

In all of this be open to uncovering the blind spots you are unaware of. Keeping an open mind is easier said than done, but consider that you reached out because you trust and respect someone else's experience.

A slightly different approach to help identify and overcome potential decision-making blind spots includes asking experts to review your thought process by going over your assumptions with you. The aim is to identify key information that you may have overlooked. This is based on the premise that it is very hard to have reviewed every conceivable perspective on a critical decision for the company.

Asking for advice is a sign of strength

I learned from experience that one of the most expensive mistakes a decision-maker can make is to think that you know it all. Looking for help is a strength, not a sign of weakness. After months and years of asking for advice to uncover blind spots and to improve the quality of plans and ideas I came to appreciate the increased quality of decision-making.

Asking for expert advice, especially those whom you consider great decision-makers will shed light on your thought process and will uncover blind spots you previously ignored. However, do keep Law #7 in mind; that at the end of the day, it is *you* who gets to decide.

- CHAPTER 9 -

Navigate with open eyes

Get feedback and correct course

"Constantly think about what you've done and how you could be doing it better." –Elon Musk

Former NASA astronaut Jim Lovell was the command module pilot of Apollo 8 and became one of the first three humans to fly to and orbit the Moon in 1968. Fifteen years before that, as a naval aviator, he was assigned to *Composite Squadron Three*, an aircraft carrier group based in California. Six months into his training he was tasked with performing his first night-time carrier landing, off the coast of Japan. Lovell was piloting a single-seat jet fighter and searching for the USS Shangri-La carrier. However, something unexpected happened: the lamp he brought on board to illuminate the cockpit accidentally short-circuited his instrument panel, and he immediately lost all instruments including radio. Despite the desperate situation he found the presence of mind to notice a faint glow in the night sea: the trails of phosphorescent algae churned up in the carrier's wake, a phenomenon called bioluminescence. The signs painted on the sea were barely visible. However, Lovell used them as sorts of guiding lights to point to the landing strip on the carrier.

He corrected course and established a safe trajectory that would help him land on the carrier, which he did much to his relief.

Cybernetics

Cybernetics is a term originating from the Greek word kybernitis (κυβερνήτης) meaning steersman, helmsman, pilot, or navigator. To achieve the objective of successfully steering his jet fighter onto the USS Shangri-La carrier, Lovell had to sit with his hands on the controls while scanning for features in the horizon and watching out for obstacles. If Lovell had spotted an obstacle just to his right, for example, he would have steered left until he cleared it, but then he would need to correct the course with a series of manoeuvres, steering left and right with increasingly precise correction, so that the aeroplane is back on its desired trajectory. Being a navigator involves constantly comparing the present direction with the desired direction and applying a series of corrective measures to avoid obstacles and to arrive at the desired destination in the most efficient manner. And very importantly, the navigator must keep a close eye on the environment to pick up on all the important clues, even the faint ones, which may be vital to thriving or surviving.

Feedback is essential to systems

Feedback is one of the major concepts in systems thinking. Feedback loops are essential to every type of system, whether it is a unicellular organism, a machine, a person, or an organisation.

Norbert Wiener (1894-1964), who was a professor of mathematics at the Massachusetts Institute of Technology (MIT), is credited with being one of the first to theorise that all intelligent behaviour was the result of feedback mechanisms and that it could be simulated by machines. Wiener is considered the father of cybernetics, with wide implications for systems control, computer science, and the organisation of society among other fields.

Feedback and course correction

A decision-maker must remember that so-called-failure is part of decision-making—it is not until you embrace failure with its risks and consequences that you are tempered into a true decision-maker. And despite best efforts and experience, decision-makers still get it wrong.

Ultimately the aim is to make a greater number of decisions with desirable results consistently, while minimising the decisions that lead to undesirable outcomes. The trick is to realise quickly enough when you are going off course. Such course corrections, however big or small are embedded into the very nature of business; in the organisation, people and systems will react to outside stimuli to achieve outcomes that are consistent with organisational goals. Course corrections are essential to the lifeblood of the company.

LAW #9:

GET FEEDBACK AND CORRECT COURSE

Why Law #9?

Great decision-makers learn from their mistakes. They do so by embracing failure as a prerequisite of great decision-making and being fully open to finding alternatives to improve systems under their control.

To get accurate feedback, the decision-maker must be proactive in gathering information regarding organisational performance so that timely decisions can be made.

Feedback mechanisms may include frameworks and procedures to measure key metrics and targets so that decisions can be made accordingly. The decision-maker will then be in a better position to make the required adjustments however big or small while leveraging the previous 8 Laws.

Being agile is navigating effectively

In increasingly dynamic waters being willing and able to quickly change course is a great organisational asset. Great decision-makers will constantly scan the horizon and chart new courses with the necessary speed. The trick is first to realise you're down a wrong path and then changing direction swiftly.

This might be easier said than done, depending on the implications of a course correction. Having an agile disposition implies that you know and accept as a decision-maker that there is more than one way of doing things. Again, the idea is to adapt to failure, overcoming unexpected obstacles and plotting a new course. Adaptability is key to long-term, sustainable growth.

Some of the tips for agile decision-making in line with the feedback you receive includes noticing the patterns to increase your ability to respond in a timely manner. This form of pattern recognition will help have resources ready before an issue occurs.

Navigating with your eyes open also implies relying on other people's radars so that their input is readily tuned into the feedback from the environment. Beware of confirmation bias or groupthink, as well as other cognitive traps that can obscure your view. A signal may be interpreted in a number of ways, so make sure that your judgment is not restricted to a particular view of the world. Again, it is about navigating with eyes fully open to the full set of possibilities, without jumping into conclusions that are.

Check progress with OKRs

One way to navigate in an agile manner relates to what we previously discussed in Chapter 6, Objectives and Key Results (OKRs) and the importance of agreeing on a system for goal setting. OKRs helped us to understand where we were heading and how individual contributions fitted into the broader objectives of the company.

What we discovered is that OKRs were not only useful for making great decisions but also for helping us gauge progress and to navigate as an organisation. Since, in the OKR framework, key results must be measurable, we were quickly able to spot if we were not achieving our targets. OKRs helped us navigate, scanning the horizon for progress and steering towards more desirable courses of action.

Managing Consultant Matthew Heusser points out that objectives provide a vision for what needs to come (the "what"), while allowing the team to decide how to get there. That means teams can focus on responding to change instead of following a plan, and they will be judged by their outcome according to some standard, not according to schedule conformance.

The nature of OKRs allows you and the team flexibility to react to your customers, so that you may correct the course as needed. However, the larger the organisation, the more difficult this will prove to be as more people need to agree on the new direction to take.

Measure customer satisfaction

Talking constantly to people, especially to customers, is a practice we have embraced; it has transformed the way we do business. We have learned that customer feedback can help us to not only learn from our mistakes but to reinforce what works well.

Not being afraid of talking to customers is something I would recommend every decision-maker. Opening channels of communication can significantly influence the quality of the feedback that you receive, improving your capacity to steer the ship in the right direction. "It is better to be critiqued and improve the idea than to fail spectacularly," says Opstera co-founder and CEO Paddy Srinivasan.

Relying *only* on instinct

While relying on experience and instincts may serve decision-makers well most of the times, solely doing so can prove to be a recipe for disaster. This can be so because previous success can create an internal image of infallibility, and the decision-maker stops accepting feedback. This problem is like closing your eyes and navigating blind—you think that the lighthouse is 500 metres to your right when in fact it is right in front of you, and that is not great—especially when you're going very fast.

Feedback can be sought via surveys, focus groups, sheer observation, advanced analytics, customer service, communities, digital channels, but perhaps the best way, whenever possible, is face to face.

It is important to keep eyes (and ears) open so that you don't stop seeking, listening, and learning from feedback. Being receptive to feedback is a true sign of seasoned decision-makers.

Remaining open to complexity

Perhaps one of the most critical applications of the cybernetic model in relation to decision-making was achieved by John D. Steinbruner, author of "The Cybernetic Theory of Decision: New Dimensions of Political Analysis". Steinburner suggested three criteria for identifying complex problems:

> *the content of the decision will affect at least two values that have trade-off relations, meaning that realising one value comes at the expense of the other;*

> *the decision is made under conditions of uncertainty, meaning a state of imperfect correlation between knowledge and the environment;*

> *the authority to take the decision is scattered among several individual players or organizational units.*

Steinbruner questions the ability to successfully handle complex decision-making under such criteria. He posits that, in order to make decision-making more manageable, decision-makers may avoid exposing themselves to all relevant information and they may discard certain information as "non-preferred" or "irrelevant".

This may lead to complex problems, not being adequately assessed by all relevant parties. In practice this might mean that problems could be "dismantled" into sub-problems that are treated separately. However, this fragmented approach to complex problem solving and decision-making may not serve the interests of the organisation.

In the interest of simplification, a significant amount of data and key relationships between stakeholders may be lost, limiting the ability of the decision-maker to see the big picture. It would be sensible to keep eyes fully open and to avoid making assumptions before correcting course.

Keep eyes open and correct course

In the MIT Sloan Management article titled "Should You Build Strategy Like You Build Software?", NY Times bestselling author Keith R. McFarland argues that strategy can only capture a company's best thinking at a given point in time. It follows that, not unlike software development, the strategy needs to be improved with the feedback received from the environment, also as the decision-makers—and the organisation as a whole—become more experienced. Given this reality, decision-making must be prepared to adapt the strategy quickly and iteratively.

The difficulty lies in knowing when to decide: neither too slowly or too quickly, processing as much information as possible and not overly simplifying data inputs.

This is especially difficult when things break down in the *cockpit*, and all you can do is look out the window trying to pick up on faint signals far below, in the ocean. Often time the decision-maker will have to fly blind one way or the other; information will never be perfect, but still, you will be tasked with making a decision to correct the course.

CHAPTER 10

Don't kill the golden goose

Care well for your ability to make great decisions

"Taking care of myself doesn't mean 'me first.'
It means 'me, too." — L.R. Knost

A cottager and his wife had a goose that laid a golden egg every day. They supposed that the goose must contain a great lump of gold in its inside, and in order to get the gold, they killed it. Having done so, they found to their surprise that the goose differed in no respect from the other geese. The foolish pair, thus hoping to become rich all at once, deprived themselves of the gain of which they were assured day by day. -The Goose that Laid the Golden Eggs, Aesop's Fables.

Great decisions are the proverbial golden eggs as per Aesop's Fables. In the quest to collect more and more eggs we get greedy: we want more customers and more profit, we want to achieve goals and reach them faster. The problem is that it is very easy—and costly—to it at the expense of the golden goose—our own health. Decision-makers can be tempted to put enormous and unhealthy amounts of pressure, forgetting that the body and namely the brain is the source of the golden eggs—of great decisions.

The capacity for making great decisions can be killed, or severely impaired, when, like the cottager and his wife, we aim to collect all the golden eggs at once, instead of taking care of the goose that lays them. As we will explore, decision-making is a tiring process which depletes mental energy.

Decision fatigue

Decision fatigue refers to the diminishing quality of decisions—the more decisions you make, the poorer the quality of these, after a long day of decision-making, for example.

In a fascinating essay by social psychologist Roy F. Baumeister and New York Times science columnist John Tierney titled "Do You Suffer From Decision Fatigue?" the authors discuss the origin and impact of decision fatigue.

They point out that "no matter how rational and high-minded you try to be, you can't make decision after decision without paying a biological price. It's different from ordinary physical fatigue—you're not consciously aware of being tired—but you're low on mental energy."

The authors highlight that the more choices you make throughout the day, the harder each one becomes for your brain, resulting in the decision-maker opting for one of two shortcuts: making more impulsive decisions instead of pondering all the potential consequences; or opting for doing nothing, that is, kicking the proverbial can down the street. Neither of these options is necessarily in the best interest of the decision-maker.

The more technical name for decision fatigue is ego depletion, a term coined by Roy F. Baumeister. His research points out to a finite reserve of mental energy—willpower—as decision-makers attempt to exercise self-control. Numerous experiments have proven that beyond being an empirical observation, willpower is indeed a depletable resource, a form of mental energy that can be exhausted; and decision-making drains it. Once you're mentally depleted, it becomes harder to consider all the different aspects and implications of various courses of action, a feeling of overwhelm. "Willpower is like a muscle," explains Roy F. Baumeister. If over-taxed, our bodies seek to conserve energy, and even seemingly simple decisions become complicated.

In such a depleted state, the decision-maker is more vulnerable to making errors of judgment. This is confirmed in experiments by Stanford professor Jonathan Levav, who demonstrated that once decision fatigue sets in, people tended to settle for recommended options, but not necessarily optimal ones.

LAW #10:

CARE WELL FOR YOURSELF, THE SOURCE OF GREAT DECISIONS

Why Law #10?

You, the decision-maker, are the source of great decisions for your company.

Decision fatigue, anxiety, sleep deprivation and burnout, among others, are some of the conditions that can severely impair or altogether kill your ability to make great decisions.

By taking good care of yourself, you will avoid jeopardising the company's position by minimising the risk of making potentially reckless decisions.

A focus on being and keeping well physically, emotionally, mentally is paramount to enabling a healthy mind able to cope with the demands of decision-making. In addition, the decision-maker will know when it is best *not* to decide, waiting for a more appropriate time.

Burnout

Burnout is a more extreme version of decision fatigue. It has been recognised by the World Health Organisation as a medical condition arising from chronic workplace stress that has not been properly managed. According to mental health and wellness guide HelpGuide, it is a "state of emotional, physical, and mental exhaustion caused by excessive and prolonged stress. It occurs when you feel overwhelmed, emotionally drained, and unable to meet constant demands".

Burnout can be associated with a number of highly debilitating emotions and other mental health conditions that can impair cognitive performance and leave a person vulnerable to illness.

Tech burnout has been described as the "dark side of working in technology". According to one survey conducted by TeamBlind, approximately 57 per cent of tech workers surveyed reported feeling burnt out. Another poll conducted by Kronos Incorporated and Future Workplace found that almost half of human resource leaders identified employee burnout for 20 to 50 per cent of their annual workforce turnover. And a third study conducted at the Yale University Centre for Emotional Intelligence showed that around 20 per cent of "highly engaged" employees are at risk of burnout.

Of relevance is that it can significantly damage the ability for great decision-making. Organisations cannot function properly, and great decisions cannot be made if decision fatigue and burnout are not addressed. But there are other behaviours which are connected to these issues.

The impact of sleep deprivation

To better understand the sometimes catastrophic effects of sleep loss on decision-making, researchers from the Kennedy Krieger Institute in Baltimore, MD, US investigated the effects of sleep deprivation on 26 participants between the ages of 22 and 40. The participants took part in the study lasting six consecutive days and nights in a controlled laboratory environment with continuous behavioural monitoring. Half of the participants were subjected to sleep deprivation, while the other half served as the control group.

Researchers observed that the sleep-deprived subjects had difficulty with initial learning of go and no go stimuli sets where subjects were instructed to respond rapidly to stimuli (pressing a button) and had severe difficulties adapting to unexpected changes. Sleep-deprived subjects also showed attentional lapses.

Researchers concluded that sleep deprivation is particularly problematic for decision-making involving uncertainty and unexpected changes in circumstances. Sleep deprivation may result in cognitive impairment, for example in emergency response, disaster management and other dynamic real-world settings with uncertain outcomes and imperfect information.

The impact of anxiety on decision-making

Another connected issue is dealing with anxiety in the workplace and its effect on decision-making. Researchers from the Center for Neuroscience at the University of Pittsburgh, PA, US conducted a study to explain how anxiety disengages the pre-frontal cortex (PFC). The PFC is the part of the brain that is essential to sound decision-making; its functions include planning, the processing of thoughts logically and rationally and considering all potential consequences of a decision. The PFC also helps calm the amygdala, part of the "reptilian brain", which runs on instinct, impulse and raw emotion, including fear.

In the controlled studies, rats—which share many physiological and biological similarities with humans—received a low dose of an anxiety-inducing drug, and in such condition, they were prompted to make decisions that would lead to the rat obtaining a sweet reward.

Researchers observed that the anxious rats made a lot more mistakes. Researchers concluded that "anxiety diminishes rule-based guidance of behaviour, leading to performance bias, and increased error propensity in decision making under conflict". In other words, anxiety reduces the brain's capacity to screen out distractions, including physical or environment distractions, or distractions in the form of thoughts and worries. Anxiety shortcircuits the brain's ability to ignore distractions by numbing neurons in the pre-frontal cortex involved in decision-making.

Sweet decisions

An unexpected area related to decision fatigue has to do with the availability of glucose in a person's bloodstream. Dartmouth researcher Todd Heatherton experimented with glucose or the lack of it in connection to willpower. His experiments proved that the availability of glucose for the brain was key to enabling the brain to restore its capacity to exercise willpower and make decisions. His research explains that the brain does not stop working when glucose is low but that "it responds more strongly to immediate rewards and pays less attention to long-term prospects."

After performing a lab task requiring self-control, people tend to eat more candy but not other kinds of salty or fatty snacks, for example. The mere expectation of having to exert self-control makes people hunger for glucose, that is reach for sweets.

Knowing when *not* to decide

According to Baumeister "Good decision making is a state that fluctuates." His studies show that people with the best self-control are the ones who structure their lives to conserve willpower. This is consistent with Laws 5, 6 and 8 recommending that the decision-maker focus mostly on the strictly necessary so that more energy is available for decision-making. "Instead of counting on willpower to remain robust all day, [decision-makers] conserve it so that it's available for emergencies and important decisions."

If you are sleep deprived, if your glucose is low, if you are anxious and/or if you are experiencing burnout you are very likely to make decisions that would negatively impact you and your company. In such a state, it would be highly undesirable to make important decisions. It would be much better to wait as long as possible to restore the energy necessary for proper decision-making.

Sharpen the saw

In his best-seller *The 7 Habits of Highly Effective People*, Stephen Covey highlights the importance of "sharpening the saw", that is of staying sharp which means preserving and enhancing the greatest asset you have—yourself. It encourages achieving a balance in life, including physical, social, emotional, and mental. Covey points out that this principle of renewal elicits an upward spiral of growth and change, of continuous improvement.

Deciding while exhausted can backfire

I recall that, after especially tough weeks of meetings full of complex problem solving and decision-making, I felt exhausted. I then realised how important it was to wind down and take care of myself physically and mentally by resting, exercising, and eating well.

I finally got the need for work-life balance and understood that working excessively at a very limited state of mental capacity is not only counterproductive for a decision-maker but that it can severely backfire. This happened after I replied to a customer email late at night with a less than a fully thoughtful response. When I re-read my email the next morning, I was shocked at what I had written and quickly re-wrote the email and rang the customer to apologise. I vowed to never write an email when I was feeling so tired.

For the sake of my ability to make great decisions, I decided that, after particularly intense stretches of work or projects that would go overtime, that I would make it a point to get as much rest as possible. I committed to purposeful rest and replenishment.

Decide early in the day

Before I studied my decision-making process, I would make relatively important decisions at any time of the day, including late in the evenings when I was closer to mental exhaustion. More often than not, when I reviewed those decisions I would think that a number of improvements could have been made. So I stopped deciding late into the evening altogether and waited at least until the next morning.

First, it was surprising to see how a night's rest can make such a positive difference in clearing the mind. The signs of exhaustion had disappeared and addressing problems and making decisions seemed easier.

I learned that neglecting sleep, exercise and poor food had a negative impact on my ability to make great decisions, so I started taking better care of myself.

Keeping in Touch

Dear reader, I hope you have enjoyed reading this book as much as I have enjoyed sharing my experience and insight with you. I hope you can apply the ten laws to help make many great decisions in your business.

Please do not hesitate to reach out to me, I would love to hear from you and I would be delighted to help with any business decision you may have.

https://www.facebook.com/OliverSurdival
Twitter @Oliver_Surdival

Notes

Ten Laws of Great Decision-Making

Ten Laws of Great Decision-Making

www.ingramcontent.com/pod-product-compliance
Lightning Source LLC
Chambersburg PA
CBHW030713220526
45463CB00005B/2021